TIME PARTICLES

Other books by Solee MacIsaac
Joy Shared
A Beloved Speck in the Universe
Little Wisdoms
Zen Days, Zen Nights
Harvest
Songs of Immortality
Soul Blossoms
Amuse-Bouches
Omens

Time Particles

Solee MacIsaac

MMXXVI

Book Design:

William Bentley

INTRODUCTION

Time Particles contains musings on our subjective experience of moment by moment being. And some stretch into subtle areas of thought about eternity. As always, it is up to the reader to assess and decide its value. From my standpoint, contemplating time was rewarding.

Solee MacIsaac

This small tome is dedicated to the invisible beings that aid my efforts. Without whom nothing would have been written. Endlessly, Thank You.

Timeless beauty
Awaits
Within.

TIME PARTICLES

Time is so strange,
It alters us
Without movement.

Love enters my being
So tenderly,
And fills all the empty spaces.

Love flows,
And all else
Falls away.

There is no
You and me,
There is only love.

If the moment
Is eternal,
Where is past and future?

If past and future are static,
The present moment
Is a light moving over a surface.

How kind everyone is,
Love circulates
Within us.

Mistakes happen.
Stress does not need
To accompany them.

Grace bestowed,
Beyond comprehension
And gratitude.

Worthiness,
Difficult to determine,
Amazing to contemplate.

Life continues,
Even when we leave it:
Perpetual motion machine.

Life forms,
Extravagantly odd,
So peculiar.

While body
Pins us down,
Mind roams freely.

Efficiency of form,
Elegant,
Simple.

One thought
Clings to another,
  Poets' love flows forth.

A room full of love,
Harmonious,
  Beautiful.

Shift from foot to foot,
Timelines waver.
  What if I hadn't...

The nowness of here,
Makes all else
Imagination.

The clock ticking
Is only arithmetic,
Time is outside of here.

Space-time construct,
Mind of God,
Unblemished reality.

Death a marker,
Limiting
This turn.

The fount of remembrances
Has run dry,
New etching begins.

The parade of moments.
Hypnotic illusion:
"Plenty of time."

Time and memory
Move in opposite
Directions.

Memory:
A window
To glimpse eternity.

Among us,
Internal forces
Flow together.

Love leaves
Nothing
Out.

Real Self
Loves
Small body self.

Movement into Autumn,
Cool, dark, quiet
Slumber.

Thoughts recorded,
Marks on a page,
Hibernate in a book.

Hearth ablaze,
Curled up cat
Twitches in dreams.

Wet, cool, meltdown,
Seasons revolve
Around the globe.

The need of us is great,
To be here, available:
Vehicles of love.

Family bonds,
Invisible ties
To a greater love.

How simple
To be
Yourself.

Ultimate privilege:
Life
In time.

Dancing fingers
Make the piano
Sing.

Perpetual light
From beyond
Is the way out of darkness.

What is up
Is down,
Stagger home.

The earth spins,
Each turn
A miracle.

If in time, I am old,
Then am I young,
In smiles.

Breathe,
Things will be,
And so will we.

Nothing is
Forever,
Time cleanses all.

Somehow it's reassuring,
That the trees are still there
Even when it's dark.

The garden of Earth
Provides for many
At no charge.

Throughout millennia
Growth, decay, change,
Yet one true thing remains.

In the blessed light
True Self
Is revealed.

We, God splinters,
Gather together
To commune our light.

Respect your life,
A gift,
Of immeasurable worth.

A line of ancestors
Stretches behind
This present You.

Laughter and joy
Surround the saddened,
Touching not a hair.

Quiet, calm, twilight
Nurtures long thought,
Brings oneself to one's Self.

Lessons teach
The humble,
Deflate the arrogant.

The body drops,
The soul
        Rises.

Raising the dead,
Returns one
        From imagination.

Obedience
To higher intelligence
        Is right order.

The bright beam
Of connection
Fuels our highest exertions.

Words: succinct,
Attention: focused,
Love: strong.

We do not know our strengths
Or weaknesses without
Right touch at right time.

God speaks,
All is accomplished,
All is done.

The light within
Guides the seeker
Home.

Even though time
Is an illusion,
Many "nows" are experienced.

This same moment
Deepens
In time.

Love repairs
The ragged edges
Of experience.

Young and old
At once;
Timeless living.

Joining the eternal
Relieves
   Time sequence.

Leaves fall,
Preparation
   For next renewal.

Time is
A Möbius strip
   Of life and death.

Profound silence
Depends upon
   Sounds that frame it.

Music—
A feeling stretched
   In time from ear to heart.

Sunless daylight,
Uncreated,
   Hallows truth.

Earth's heartbeat
Is so loud that
	Only angels can endure.

Time,
Is what happens
	Between two moments.

Healing transpires
When floodgates open
	To endless light.

Sequence of tones:
Simplistic description
Of the miracle we call music.

Breathing through
One's navel
Signals coming birth.

Many things are strange,
None so much
As your very Self.

Mysteries exist
Before and after
We do.

Each focused moment
Teaches something
Immense and unique.

Yearning
For what is not here, now,
Is a death wish.

With one voice
We aspire to the source,
With profound gratitude.

It takes no time
To experience beauty,
To enjoy existence.

All that I have,
All that I am,
Is due to You.

We live in time,
But timeless love
Sustains us.

Together,
We are a living tribute
To prolonged prayer.

Thanksgiving:
Hearts synchronize
In blissful rhythm.

There are two seasons
On most of Earth,
    And two transitions.

In some places,
There is only
    Summer or Winter.

Changes don't stop
But modulate
    Differently.

Being is change,
Continuous motion,
Even in death.

Surfaces provide
The illusion
Of separateness.

The canyons of being
Have long shadows,
Climb up to unity.

Eat up the world,
One gulp at a time,
Until you are filled with light.

Eyes perceive external light,
Inner eye perceives
Inner light.

Drifting will not arrive,
Focusing contains more
Possibilities.

Awareness in a moment,
More valuable
Than golden dreams.

Sunlight through
Red rose petals;
Food for angels.

Our needs are simple,
The pendulum of wants
Disturbs equilibrium.

Our highest wish
Is to know the source
Of our fate.

Love is the force
That pulls us to
Ourselves.

Time hardly exists,
In this eternal
Now.

Limited Time
Does not know
Eternity.

Love unites
Mortal
With eternal.

Light!
Do we really know
What you are?

Order,
In the sequence of things,
    Prevails in the universe.

If we put our foot down,
We must lift it again,
    To dance.

The travesty of life
Isn't in war and death.
    It is in missing the point.

Make your plan,
Then experience
Each unfolding moment.

Kindness from the heart
Heals many wounds,
Freshens foul air.

Content within one's Self
Brings the freedom to notice
Needs of others.

The silver flame
Of Oneness
    Radiates a sphere of light.

Our brains are not
Designed to manipulate
Zeros and ones.

Watching from outside,
Time is a frozen
    Landscape of moments.

Movement,
Plus time,
Equals biological existence.

To be grateful
Is the payment
And the reward.

There is time enough
To be here,
To know ourselves.

In the end
We will know
The beginning.

Disaster:
It would not happen,
If it was not needed.

Beyond luck,
Our time
Is counted.

Rising up together,
We break the time
Ceiling.

Grateful for our life,
Sets the right tone
For incoming lessons.

Without memory
We would burn ourselves
Again in the same fire.

Love is the source,
The means,
     And—the destination.

It all comes down to
Recognizing
     Who You are.

This time, that time,
My time, your time,
     Every time, no time.

The moment deepens
When we
Arrive to meet it.

By what we are shown
The possibilities
Narrow within us.

Joy in life
Is the opportunity
To love.

I did not choose to be me,
But someone chose me
To Be.

Tree lights,
Shining by the doorstep.
Step out into Winter.

In moments,
The endless light
Is far beyond happiness.

Precious time,
Irretrievable,
Impossible to evaluate.

Days, hours, minutes,
This moment,
Not graspable.

All that is
Necessary,
Resides within.

Realization
Is
Timeless.

Movement
Through time
Is an illusion.

Everything
Is already here
Right now.

Truly accepting
This moment,
Reveals Self.

The timeless light
Always
Exists.

Living is a state
Of mind
And being.

Death is a privilege
Earned throughout
Life.

A water drop
Enters a pond,
No longer a drop.

How long it takes
Depends
On who's counting.

Time is a flexible
Extension
   Of elastic space.

Love is the great
Timeless connector
   Through all mediums.

Symbols warm
A longing heart;
   Not a substitute for reality.

Light-filled eyes
See more,
Understand more.

No matter how beautiful,
The visible
Is far less than the invisible.

Hidden in plain sight,
Strings are pulled
Behind the scene.

Seeing
Has many
Levels.

Time and Will
Play a part
In penetrating the unseen.

Beauty may be blissful,
Better to stay
Home first.

Ignorance
Will not save
The naive.

To see beneath the words
Dive deep,
Don't hold your breath.

We are not here
For comfort,
But to be shown reality.

Even a strong
Fear-lock
　　Is an illusion.

The way out
Is always
　　Toward the light.

The body
Is not the enemy,
　　Nor the friend.

Real change,
Though seeming cathartic,
        Comes moment by moment.

By doing
What we do not wish,
        An unseen agenda is disrupted.

God
Is simply
        Present existence.

The law of time
Is designed to slow down
Seeing all events at once.

Don't believe your eyes,
Tricksters are everywhere.
Love and be content.

Uncreated light
Does not need
A witness.

Your radiance
Transcends
Time.

We follow
What pleases us,
Duty requires alternate route.

Consciousness
Is all
There is.

The face of God
Is the face
Behind yours.

Time after time
We are lucky
To be.

This moment
In time,
Is everything.

Love is my aim,
Love is my fuel,
Love is my gift.

Seeing with love,
Hearing with open heart,
We are Presence.

The heart is flexible;
No matter how many times
It is broken, it beats on.

Don't worry about
What is left behind,
Nothing real is ever lost.

Transformation,
Is grace
Under fire.

This Midnight
Marks another
Revolution around the Sun.

Nothing is missing,
It's an all-inclusive life;
You are the pearl in the oyster.

Right in front of you
Is everything
You could want or need.

Flames rise
In timeless glory,
Transmuting energy.

We owe more
Than we can pay,
      Love and gratitude is key.

We don't count miseries,
We count
      Loves.

It is easier to
Love,
      Than to resist.

Time frames
Each individual
Experience.

Love
Turns time into
Eternity.

The art form
Of our life
Is depicted in time.

To walk in love-light
Is to be
Thrice blessed.

Disappointment
Pierces
Expectations.

Heart-seeing
Reveals
Mysteries.

Love circulates
Among those
Joined in presence.

Real freedom
Has never
Been lost.

We are not trapped in time,
The door has been open
All along.

Creations come through you,
But they are not
Yours.

The familiar person
Is also not
You.

Sing the prophecy
Of each moment,
Tone by tone.

The senses
Are glorious gifts
Of great privilege.

To stretch time,
Wait,
In a line.

To leave time,
Quietly enter
The sacred space.

Joy in life,
Lasts longer
Shared.

The force of love
Increases
Angelic joy.

Blessed light
Greets,
Open hearts.

The canyons
Of the heart,
Hold secret longings.

We surgically divide
Time,
Into minutes and seconds:

Like boundaries
Of countries,
Imaginary to the globe.

Friends together
Hold open doorways to
    Confluence of light.

Pre-Spring hints
Tantalize
    Frozen ground.

Bright Sun:
A little warms
    Frosty boot prints.

Into the mix
Of yes and no,
New possibilities arise.

Sounds are vibrations;
Conscious listening
Educates reverberations.

We are
What
We seek.

By sharing,
All are
Enhanced.

Time has boundaries,
Love
Has none.

A cherubic smile,
Better received
Than a sagacious frown.

A moment of laughter
Can lessen
An hour of sorrow.

Seasons reveal
Changes are
Cyclical.

Cycles seem
Directionless,
Until we realize the spiral.

The inner meaning of time
Is shown
    Outside its perimeter.

Waves of light
Shimmer over
    Endless depths of ocean.

Another full moon face
Lights another night
    Of Winter's frigid seclusion.

Before and after,
Neither satisfies
Like Now.

Deeper into
Presence,
Time is inconsequential.

Cabbage soup simmering,
Ready in 30 minutes;
Cooking is timing.

Kittens look soft and sweet,
But have very
   Sharp claws.

Awareness is forged
Into greater being
   By absorbing finer energies.

Fuel for consciousness
Is always
   Everywhere.

Only now
Can presence
Exist.

New discoveries
Bring new energy
From stored recesses.

The most real
In this world,
Is the most subtle.

Sort, classify,
Organize;
And always absorb.

There is
Nothing
We cannot use.

We are always
Awake
If we choose it.

Breaths and heartbeats
Keep perfect
Earth time.

Deep in the well
Of Time
Lay many mysteries.

Our speech
Does not accommodate
Our state.

Amazing to have to make
An effort to leave
What we do not like.

Slow is fast,
Fast is slow,
Time is senseless.

Eons carry on in cosmos time,
Our diminutive scale
Experiences only moments.

Sentiment
Is no substitute
For real emotion.

Self-realization
Melts
Boundaries.

Awareness
Really is,
Always Here.

A heartbeat,
A breath,
An impression.

A red rose,
A shining moment,
Love-filled sweetness.

Generations before
And after;
Only this moment exists.

Living in time,
We know only past moments,
And seeds of future.

Time is understood,
Until you try
To explain it.

It is a miracle
That we
Exist.

Even Greenwich
Can't keep up
    With capricious Time.

    Ephemeral moments,
Though fleeting—
    Precious and eternal.

    Sharing time together,
A special privilege
    Not always appreciated.

Time is an abstraction
Until you are
    Running behind your bus.

Illusion of Time
Is difficult to break;
    Requires a leap into Reality.

There is no
Present moment,
    Without a present witness.

To reveal our true Selves
Through time,
　　Many falsities are endured.

Shedding the unreal
Is a lifetime
　　Of suffering.

How strange
Is our life,
　　How strange to Be.

Without love
There is
No being.

Love is the
Medium
Of existence.

Illness and healing
Resolve in time,
With chicken soup.

When planning,
Intervals must be
Considered.

Open your heart
Of heart,
Sing full throated.

All in good time,
God's time,
Is all.

It seems things
Are hidden in time,
But not in eternity.

Nothing is hidden,
Shadowed, or lost
In reality.

Because God
Is all,
How could it not be so.

Sometimes it seems,
Living the same moment
Over and over.

Joining the eternal
Now,
We are never alone.

A brilliant column of light
Stands continuously
Without shadows.

What is it,
That stops love
Flowing through you?

When you love,
You see how loved
Everything is.

We need help,
And help is here,
Even when not recognized.

Divisions of time,
Fostered by breath,
Tenacious illusion.

The Sun is
Always warming the Earth,
Even when she hides her face.

Flower petals drop,
Autumn, winter, happen
Before blooms begin again.

Persephone had to visit
The Underworld every year,
To pay for Summer.

It's no use complaining,
Payment
Will be extracted.

The ultimate prize
Is our very
Self.

If it ever
Will happen,
It already has.

Love, luck,
Destiny, time,
The package is complete.

Be kind,
We are the beginning
And the end.

We are born into time,
And die to leave it.
What is before and after?

If space and time are linked,
Is before and after
No space?

Trusting to love
What is not understood,
Creates a growth medium.

When soul enters
The body,
    Invisible meets visible.

Light is enclosed
By the dark body,
    Until it is strong enough.

Remember, when arguing,
You are speaking
    To God.

The ticking clock
Is no measure
Of True meter.

Raindrops on roof,
Musical cadence
From heaven.

Each moment
Offers up
Its unique intensity.

Verdant intrusion,
Spring has painted
The landscape.

Digging in the ground,
Each particle of earth
Is a promise to Spring.

Plant a seed;
Make a wish
Come true.

Love carries the day,
The hour, the minute,
This very second.

Galaxy time, light years;
Sun time, eons;
Earth time, centuries.

In our lives,
One moment seems
To outweigh all the rest.

A small particle of time
May be a concept,
But isn't really a thing at all.

Time allows sequential events
To proceed in harmonious
Love-Light.

Grateful and humbled,
Being here,
Smiling.

Each second
Is worthy
Of attention.

Walking in Earth's garden,
Every creature
Shines with life-light.

Death doesn't solve
Life's problems,
But resolves an older debt.

Humor can reveal
Weak points
In our opinions.

True intelligence
Cannot be determined
By retention of facts.

Every vessel carries
A God spark—though
Unaware and unvalued.

That which is real
Harbors
　No fantasy.

At times,
Payment is made
　Long before reward.

Deliver up
Your worst fears
　And all your woes.

Earth tremors are reminders
Of the sleeping giant
Beneath our feet.

Time is counted.
Who does the counting?
What is the right amount?

Time flies,
Too much or not enough;
Difficult to master.

Strange melody
In rain pattern
Quiets the soul.

Music and Time
Seem
Unequivocally connected.

What music
Can angels hear
In Eternity?

Time defines life
And gives it
    Boundaries.

If everything that can happen
Has already happened,
    What are we doing here?

When contemplating
Meaning,
    Don't leave out the invisible.

Even though age takes its toll,
Clear presence
    Remains unblemished.

Words and syllables
Have meter and magic;
    Stillness and silence excel.

A journey in time
Is called
    A life.

Though we are far apart
In Space,
    We are joined in Time.

    A meticulous arrangement
Of tones can create
    A symphonic masterpiece.

    Without love,
No sounds
    Are beautiful.

Geometric precision
Erects majestic temples
   Flowing from the mind of God.

We lift each other up
In each moment
   Of uncreated light.

Living in time
Is a closed box
   Compared to reality.

Every minute particle
Of our experience
	Holds a meaningful key.

Snow! Covering green,
A billowing bridal veil
	Of pure white.

Spring's
Backward looking
	Joke.

In subjectivity
We lose many
Opportunities.

Time reversal,
Is it the same as
Memory?

The still point
Is not bothered
By time's cacophony.

A drop of water,
A blade of grass,
Neon green appears.

Time is flexible,
But procrastination
Will not grant more time.

Pure awareness,
A window from one world
To another.

To change the past,
Turn time inside out,
Before washing.

A mind focused on
Giving creative love
Radiates a shining halo.

Time is a burden
To those waiting,
A respite for lovers.

Spring growth process
Is a time emblem
Sublime.

New bonnet, new shoes,
Flowers abound;
Parade is about to commence.

Spring cleaning
Makes space
For new lessons.

Leave your boots
At the door step,
Humbly enter sacred space.

Crocus, daffodils, jonquils;
Adornments
For Persephone's return.

Put away old habits,
Erase tired thoughts and fears,
A new era has begun.

Presence with no dips
Or troughs:
Infinite unblemished light.

Digging into history,
Though much is repeated,
Presence is always unique.

Spring's colors and fragrance
Overwhelm:
A blissful shock.

Inevitable time
Persists in infinite,
    Earthbound commitment.

Each heavenly body
Has its own
    Ordered time schedule.

Earth's well of gravity
Makes time sluggish;
    Freed-up time soars.

Practice on everything
And everyone,
Ultimately love your Self.

Uncreated light
Is love
Focused.

Riding the body wave,
Enjoying
Spring's new clothing.

To be a leaf in the wind,
Detach
From static holds.

At times,
Everything you know
Holds you back.

There is more than enough
Time
To penetrate truth.

To move with change,
Let go of possessions
And time restraints.

How to live
Is always
The question.

Some secrets
Are not hidden
At all.

A passing cloud
Makes one grateful
For Sunlight.

Time may be unlimited;
Our lives are not.
Wasting time is expensive.

New growth
Covers old mistakes
On twisted vines.

Death
Is closer
  Than anticipated.

In our modest
Three dimensions,
  Stars look like pretty lights.

Sweeping trails
Of white vapor
  Follow a roaring jet.

White sky drops
Cold blanket
Covering weeping buds.

One step forward,
Two backward,
Start again.

Time for pleasure,
Time for pain,
Time to accept with gratitude.

Cold snow outside,
Hot fireplace inside;
	Cherish Winter's last gasp.

Friction is only denying force
If it's used;
	Otherwise it's wasted difficulty.

Like the pyramid
Of consciousness,
	We are together at the top.

Service
Is a marker
Of evolution.

Open all words,
So love
Flows freely.

No beginning,
No ending;
God is, "Yes."

Throughout time
Memory bits
Create soul life.

Psyche's many trials
Eventually gave rise
To Buddhahood.

Help from angels
Isn't just a magnificent gift,
But an ultimate necessity.

Good, bad, and indifferent;
Everything fits
Into Time's vault.

Winter's wrath
Makes Summer's pleasantries
Relished and beloved.

An hour in a glass,
A second in a thimble,
This moment—free for all.

Light splits gray clouds,
Moist green hills host
Waving daffodils.

Truth in each sequential note
Makes hearts vibrate
In harmony.

Friendship is safe harbor
In a sea of enemies.
Befriend six and four loves.

All lovers see truth
In their beloved's
Eyes.

We are mirrors
For each other,
If we know how to look.

The simplicity
Of natural elements
Is simply perfect.

The perfection
Of new birth
Is an underrated virtue.

Old age
Is a condition
Earned by Time's discretion.

The velocity of time
Depends upon
The subjective viewer.

Celebrate your life,
While it's
Yours.

The intensity of one moment
Sends out echoes that radiate
Through past and future.

Viridian fields
Glowing in Spring sunrise
Offer up white lilies.

Love all who
Enter your sphere,
   Soul-meet timing is perfect.

Infants and octogenarians
Share the energy
   Surrounding the birth-death portal.

Sunlight returns;
Reminder of the light
   That never fades.

Mayan culture
Did not view time as linear,
But as a recurring cycle.

The Maya had names
For each particle
Of time.

Falling through time,
The safety net
Is always love.

The sublime
Is nothing
If not sublimely simple.

Seeing through the eyes
Is a treasure
Easily taken for granted.

Essence glee,
Indescribable joy,
Grace young and old.

The guides
Assisting our roles
Are tireless in their efforts.

The shining orb
Of our being is blessed
Beyond comprehension.

Angelic influence
Penetrates layers
Of self-made illusion.

One lonely buttercup
To some eyes,
A bee palace.

A happy fate
Brings much more
Than pleasure.

One breaks through;
The others applaud.
The way is forged.

Connections between us
Are strong
When flooded with pure Light.

Inner quiet
Is profound
Beauty.

Fresh green leaves
Nestling tender buds
Bordering new orchard.

Puppies, kittens, chicks,
Wide-eyed
        At Spring's bounty.

Another spiral twist,
Eggs, flowers, babies:
        Fertility Season.

Time to be born,
Live and die;
        Time enough to Be.

Timing is everything,
Says anyone who
Cooks, dances, loves, works....

Moments pass me by
Till I'm fast enough
To catch them.

Be brave,
Nothing of real value
Can be lost.

Each tick of the clock
Is another gift
        For each of us.

Decisions in a moment
Are difficult,
        Without established priorities.

First day of Spring,
The birds and trees
        Know it well.

A thought, a heartbeat,
A love;
We are so small in eternity.

A short trip,
A change of scenery,
Time stretches again.

Duck dinner,
Chinese jello,
The Golden Gate Bridge.

The soaring pinnacle
Of School on Earth
        Is felt and known by few.

Time says: Forward, forward.
Memory urges: Back, back.
        Love's quiet voice: Be now.

Heaven Light
Is immediately accessible
        At all times.

Neither birth
Nor death
Can mar the Self.

Don't try to
Live forever;
Live in forever.

The untried heart and mind
Of a child
Can hold the whole world.

Relentless Time,
Burden or treasure:
A ceaseless march home.

To be beyond words,
Is the right place
To be.

Together in silence
A unified field of love
Opens wide.

It is always
The right time
To be Present.

Priorities fall into place
The moment
Presence appears.

Only with a generous heart
Can one afford
To care for many things.

To increase your possessions,
Either expand your heart,
Or reduce your inventory.

A real sunset
Can only be captured
By the eye of the heart.

Outside of time,
The clock disintegrates
In the cosmic wind.

The dark half
Knows little about the light.
The light knows everything.

Realizing past mistakes,
Need not be a gruesome task,
As it strengthens resolve.

We are given so much help,
On this inner path,
And we absolutely need it.

Pitying oneself may be justified,
But has a high cost
    And a minus value.

The birds had a meeting,
Sorry kitty,
    You were definitely not invited.

Rainy day,
Simmering soup,
    Glowing love-filled eyes.

Ill feelings aren't mandatory,
We are more
Than our circumstances.

Gracious and true,
We kneel before
All who have chosen this path.

All that was, is, will be, exists;
Then there is no time or space,
Only God.

Awareness doesn't need 'I',
'I' is much too small,
　　Only Love is large enough.

Such a privilege
To share our lives
　　With those on the path.

The fraction of a second
To capture impressions,
　　Is a fleeting opportunity.

Time is of the body;
Not so the limitless
     Realized awareness.

We are not inside
Or outside our bodies,
     Light is everywhere.

To venture outside
The moment
     Is to court death.

Formulas and institutions
Provide stable illusions,
Temporary platforms.

We interact on many levels,
Especially in the joint field
Of awareness.

Drop systematic chains,
When realization of freedom
Appears.

Stars in their courses,
Follow predictable routes:
What is their experience?

We go about our business,
Our patterns are fated.
What is our experience?

If timing is everything,
Who and when we meet
Is of prime significance.

The author
Of this play
Must smile a lot.

Vivaldi understood
Winter
In a crystalline way.

Each particle of time
Contains all possibilities
Via conscious awareness.

Humbled and grateful
We approach each other
With love and earned respect.

There is no time
Outside of life,
Outside the self.

Time is like a rubber band,
Flexible
Until it snaps.

Alarm clocks
Are a murderous
Invention.

Telling time by the stars
May not be totally accurate,
But very beautiful.

Spring cautiously
Dips her toe
Into the rain and foggy day.

Fear is not to be
Conquered,
But to be released.

What happens to us
Does not need to define us;
We are not birth or death.

A pocket full of miracles
Is the luck
Impossible to purchase.

Languid and peaceful,
Awareness
Whisks time particles away.

Lost in time
Are many questions,
And forgotten answers.

On-time dinner guests
Tread carefully
Into a sacred space.

Even though there are
No real secrets,
    Many things are still unknown.

    How is it so many useful things
Are forgotten
    From time past?

    Awareness never diminishes,
Existence is clear and open,
    Uncreated light is here.

What little of time
We can contain,
    Doesn't lie in future or past.

Life seems speeded-up,
Going too fast;
    Slowing down inside helps.

Show someone you care;
Time limits life,
    Spread love while you can.

April Fool's Day
Played quite a trick on us,
Lots of hail—but no tornado.

Adding up the moments,
Sweet, harsh, rare, or common;
In the end all are welcome.

She moves my pen,
She teaches with words,
O, Muse—all acclaim to you.

Snow-white crystals
Line tree branches,
  Shivering newborn birds.

In stressful times,
Take care of yourself
  And those around you.

All advancements
Are realized
  In small increments.

When your inner sun rises,
Nothing is more beautiful
Than the light in your eyes.

How vivid everything
Is when forever light
Outlines every surface.

Timely and succinct,
Each moment
Has its own message.

From pacemakers
To a metronomes:
        Trackers of rhythm.

Time is divided
Into beats, breaths,
        And perceptions.

A drop in the pond
Sends ringlets to the edge,
        A tone sends music to ears.

Particles of time
Release moments
Sparking consciousness.

Multiplying love
Is as easy as one plus one
Times a million.

Walt Whitman
Soared in his body,
Even when he couldn't walk.

Soul experience
In higher realms,
        Indescribably intimate.

Hungry for reality;
Deep need to immerse
        In true existence.

Without help
From our benefactors
        We are drifters in Time.

This moment
Of infinite beauty
Contains all of time and space.

Everywhere
There is light,
There is love.

A hidden jewel
Resides
In each difficult moment.

There is no escape
From lessons
    That open eyes of the heart.

Bow in gratitude
To all who show
    Yourself to your Self.

A ticking clock
Cannot know
    The depth of each moment.

Composure, clarity, awareness,
All separate,
Is re-membered.

Priorities settled,
The world
Becomes my oyster.

Water falls from the sky,
Heaven's valuable gift:
Source of life.

In a short space of time
Anything can happen;
Even a first step.

To bring artistry
To the moment,
Open inner eye.

To love,
And to create,
Not so very different.

A simple word,
Spoken with love,
Can open mighty portals.

Inner being
Of great dimension
Can flood even a city with light.

Time pockets
Are kept
In shiny gold lockets.

To grow younger
Leave the future
Behind.

In his magnificent creation
God allows vibrations
Delighting eyes and ears.

To trek the hallways
Of reality,
Buy soleless shoes.

To be nothing at all,
Cross into
Infinite freedom.

Granular time
Is only
This very moment.

West, East, North, South,
Have little meaning
On a sphere.

What happens
When lightning
Strikes the ocean?

Take a shower, make breakfast,
Another day
Is suspiciously ordinary.

Is the day
Actually ordinary?
Or, am I ordinary?

The interlocking system
Of Earth, life, time, nature,
Is exquisitely magical.

The light point
On a drop of rain,
Glistens a wink from God.

The timeframe
For this life,
Is Fate-scheduled.

Unbeknownst to us,
We are cradled in the hands
Of beatific angels.

The loving care provided
Is not for the body;
Souls are nourished.

The focused attention
Of an artist in creating,
Requires a labor of love.

When light recedes
Eyes close,
Yet nothing disappears.

A good evening has a book,
A glass of wine, and
A glowing fireplace.

Too many times
There is more craving
Than ability to maintain.

Hokusai loved
Mount Fuji
With pen and heart.

Block print artistry
Is more personal,
Than perfect camera images.

Accept every precious gift
Offered,
Each present moment.

Spring sneaks up behind
Mountains of snow,
        And gloom, gloom, gloom.

Total sun,
Green everywhere,
        And bloom, bloom, bloom.

Although childbirth
Is mechanical,
        It is no less a miracle.

In a tiny moment,
The universe appeared,
     And the time spiral began.

A grain at a time
Makes its way
     From singular to unity.

The multiple dimensions
Of Time
     Realize every futile thought.

A wild variety of fruits, vegetables,
Colors, flavors,
Make a generous banquet.

A cornucopia of nourishment
And love
Is provided in Eden's garden.

From Time immemorial,
A shower of abundance
Has followed our steps.

Tributes to the gods
Can never balance
The debt.

To witness changing times
On the world stage
Is to live history.

Children are a responsibility,
A joy, and a bitter sweet love;
Emblem of parental existence.

To help bring a soul into
A potential life,
	Is a challenging decision.

Which soul is chosen,
Can only be decided
	On a higher level.

Family is a karmic unit,
Whereby love heals and fortifies
For future lifetimes.

Life can be grim,
Happy people
Have earned contentment.

Return of the Sun
At daybreak
Releases joy and birdsong.

Our world could
Be black and white,
Color is given to value beauty.

Days, months, years, eons,
Inevitable Time proceeds;
We appear and disappear.

Love knits
The fabric of lifetimes
Together.

Day comes to the end,
As all things must,
Leaving space for rosy Dawn.

Inner silence meets
Still point awareness;
    Presence is born.

Harmonic vibrations
Please
    Ear, eye, and soul.

A master
Teaches us
    Humility.

What is most simple
Is usually
Correct.

Milestones in time
Help to track
Linear progress.

By incubating light,
We will
Birth a Sun.

The progression of time
Should not frighten us,
    We will all be together at last.

Time has a percussion sound,
Loud or soft,
    It is rhythmic.

The cycle of time
Holds compulsive dancers
    In endless arabesque.

A full moon, one vivid star,
Lights the landscape
    For the long walk home.

When love links
To your movements,
    Everything is graceful.

Sweep together
All scattered time particles,
    Preserve present moments.

The human heart
Has four chambers,
   Dispatching miraculous life.

The emotional heart,
Chamber-less, boundless
   In its capacity for loving.

Slip between particles
Of time,
   Leave everything behind.

The guarded gates
Refuse entry to anyone larger
Than a grain of time.

A gray beard
Does not guarantee
A wise thought or word.

The number of moments lived,
Cannot equal one moment
Of conscious Self-awareness.

Wearing a gloomy face
Is not graceful attire
   For meeting the gods.

Your light
And God's light
   Are the same.

Your spark from God
Is not born,
   And does not die.

Earth to earth,
Heaven to heaven;
    Words with deep meaning.

Time allotted
Is assigned before birth.
    There are no mistakes.

Ascent on the vertical scale
Is not dependent on time
    Or circumstance.

When confusion enters,
Love and presence
Supply energy for solution.

When time is up,
Put down the ball
And go home.

The way out
Of unreality,
Is to embrace the play.

For awareness to evolve,
Matter must be loved,
Limits must be seen as guides.

Now is always,
Not born,
Not dying.

Peel the banana,
Drive the truck,
Listen to the rain.

Time doesn't exist,
Space doesn't exist,
　　Likeness vibrates as one.

Dividing space and time
Enables sensations,
　　To be perceived separately.

Awareness
Does not need
　　Divisions.

Time's limitation lets us
Listen to the spheres' music
One note at a time.

Eyes or ears
Are not required
To be aware of reality.

Full sun,
Bright reflections,
Spring stalking Summer.

One sees,
All are bidden,
   Truth, love, light abound.

The storybook world
Delights, scares, astonishes,
   But won't satisfy the searcher.

Life exists for us,
By us,
   Through us.

Time dissolves
Life, memory, places,
Everything except soul.

A journey through time
May provide insight,
And a shocking sameness.

Love pouring from heaven,
Every soul
Is nourished with will to exist.

One infinite love,
One infinite light,
One infinite soul.

As time is a handy illusion,
A particle is also,
As is an individual.

Many "Me's" and "My's"
Disappear
With unfolding light.

White roses
Cascade to fountain head,
   In crystalline blue waters.

The field of awareness
Is more than individual,
   With no divisions.

To be truly present
Is to give up
   Moments.

Give up everything,
Everywhere, every when,
In glorious Love light.

Time's up!
In the end,
Is the beginning.